The Amazing Incredible Shrinking Drums

Story by Thornton Cline
Illustrations by Susan Oliver

ISBN: 978-1-57424-344-4
SAN 683-8022

Cover by James Creative Group

All Illustrations by Susan Oliver

CENTERSTREAM®

Copyright © 2017 CENTERSTREAM Publishing, LLC
P.O. Box 17878 - Anaheim Hills, CA 92817

www.centerstream-usa.com

"Thornton Cline does it again! "The Amazing Incredible Shrinking Drums" is the perfect book for every young drummer teaching two very valuable lessons, the need to practice daily and to be humble.

I've been playing drums for 45 years. I've playing and teaching professionally for over 30 years. I still practice daily and I take lessons all the time. After a lifetime of playing I still find it very challenging and rewarding. I tell all of my students no matter how good you are there is always someone who is better. There are so many rhythms, techniques and musical styles to learn that you'll never have it all. However, if you work hard, think big, and have fun you might just be a drummer in a great band some day!"

– Bart Robley, drummer for the Sam Morrison Band, Gretsch Artist, Teacher, Columnist and Author

"This book teaches a lesson more valuable than any rudiment, and it applies to any musician no matter where they are on their journey. Stay humble."

– Chris Golden, Award-winning Entertainer, multi-instrumentalist, producer, and T.V. host

"In this wonderful book, Thornton Cline has found a way to entertain and teach kids about one of life's most important music lessons – a humble heart helps you grow from the start. What a great way to educate children on their journey towards becoming great musicians...as well as great adults!"

– Evan Pollack, Experience Drums, LLC

"This book is great because not only does it teach you the importance of working hard and being aware of the talents of others, it teaches what in my opinion is life's most important lesson in any situation which is humility"

– Seth Rausch, drummer for Keith Urban

The Amazing Shrinking Incredible Drums

When Matt was eight years old, he begged his parents for a drum set.

"We'll think about it when you're older," his mom said.

But, Matt couldn't wait until he was older.

He wanted to play now.

So, he tapped cool rhythms on anything he could find: tables, pots, pans, doors, books, floors and even on people.

One day, his parents surprised him with a set of drums. Matt couldn't believe his eyes.

"Here are the drums you've been so patiently waiting for," his dad said.

"We've signed you up for some lessons with Mr. Thompson at the music store," his mom said.

"We expect you to practice every day," his dad said.

"And not to play late at night when we're sleeping," his mom said.

"You've got it!" Matt said.

Matt gave his parents a big hug.

"Thank you, Mom and Dad!" he said.

Matt's lessons with Mr. Thompson were so much fun that all Matt wanted to do was play drums.

Matt played his drums in the morning before school,
after school,

and until he had to go to bed.

One day, Matt's friends, Shawn and Conner came over to hear him play his drums.

"Watch this," Matt said proudly.

He placed his drum sticks in his hands and began to play faster and faster. He played difficult rhythms. Finally, he finished with a loud cymbal crash.

"Wow!" Conner said.

"You're really good!" Shawn said.

"I know! I'm not only good, I'm the best!" Matt shouted.

Connor and Shawn were startled by Matt's bragging words. They stood there speechless.

"I'm better than my drum teacher, and better than all the drummers out there," Matt said.

Matt's bragging made his friends not want to hang out with him. They left and went home.

All week, Matt bragged again and again about how great he was on the drums.

"You should hear me play drums. I'm the best!" Matt told his teachers at school.

"It's not polite to brag," they said. They rolled their eyes and tried to bring him back down to earth.

"I'm better than you, you and you on the drums," Matt said as he pointed his finger at his classmates.

Matt bragged so much that none of his friends or classmates wanted to be around him. They wouldn't even speak to him.

"Who does he think he is," his friends said.

One day, Matt and his dad went to a gigantic music store.

They had a large selection of drums.

A strange-looking man, dressed like a rock star was playing the drums. He was amazing. He played very difficult rhythms and at lightning speed.

When he finished playing, Matt looked at him and yawned as if he was bored.

"You don't know me, but I know a lot about you," the man said.

"Like what?" Matt replied.

"I know you like to brag about how great you are," the man said.

"That's because I am the best on the drums!" Matt replied.

The man laughed and said, "My dear boy, there will also be someone more advanced than you on the drums. So don't ever forget that."

Matt pretended not to listen.

"The more you brag about how good you are on the drums, the faster your drums will shrink until you won't be able to play them anymore," the man warned.

Matt laughed at the man and, walked away and went home with his dad.

Matt continued to brag about how great he was on the drums until one day, Matt discovered that his drum set had shrunk to the size of a miniature drum set.

He couldn't believe his eyes. His drums were tiny enough to fit inside a doll house.

Matt became worried and upset. He thought about what the strange man in the music store had said about his drums shrinking if he kept on bragging.

Could that man in the store have been telling the truth; that my drums would really shrink? Hmm.... I wonder, Matt thought to himself.

Matt began to have second thoughts about his bragging. He missed his drums. But, his tiny drum set was too small to play. He decided to stop bragging. He wondered what would happen to his drum set.

Some friends asked him how his drumming was going. "It's alright, I guess. I can always use some improvement," Matt answered.

His friends were surprised at how humble Matt seemed.

His teachers asked him about his drum playing. "It's okay. I'm going to have to work harder to play as good as some of the drummers I've seen. I've got a lot to learn," Matt said.

His teachers couldn't believe how humble Matt was.

One day, Matt noticed that his tiny drum set was growing in size. He picked up his sticks and started playing. His drum set grew bigger and bigger until it had reached its original full size. That made Matt happy again because he had missed his drums. He couldn't wait to tell his parents how excited he was.

"Mom, Dad, thank you so much for my drums. I love them!"

"You're welcome, Son. We're proud of you!" his mom and dad said.

"I found out the hard way that there may be people who are more advanced than I am, but that's okay, I shouldn't compare myself to others – I should just be the best that I can be. I'll work really hard. One day, I might become a famous drummer in a rock band!"

THE END.

Song Titles

Play My Drums

Thornton Cline

♩= 108 **Confidently**

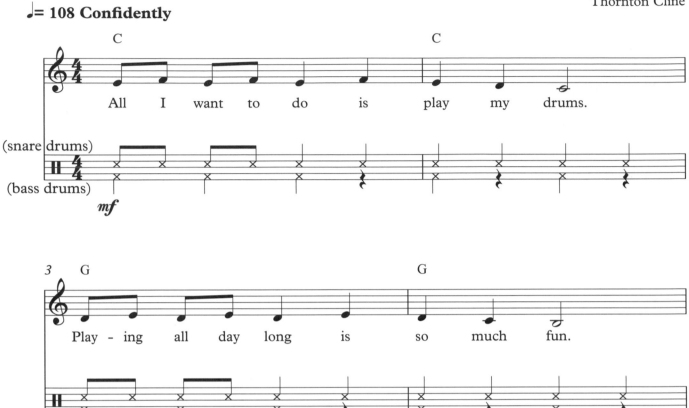

All I want to do is play my drums.

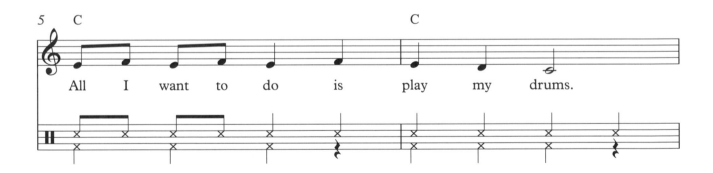

Play - ing all day long is so much fun.

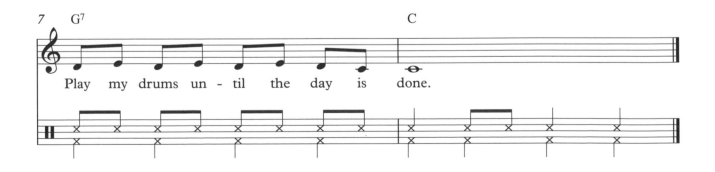

All I want to do is play my drums.

Play my drums un - til the day is done.

I'm Really Good

Thornton Cline

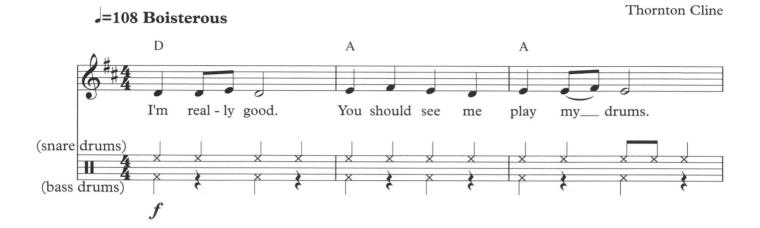

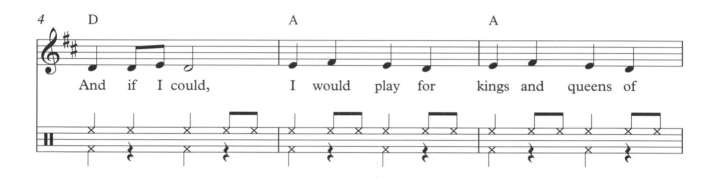

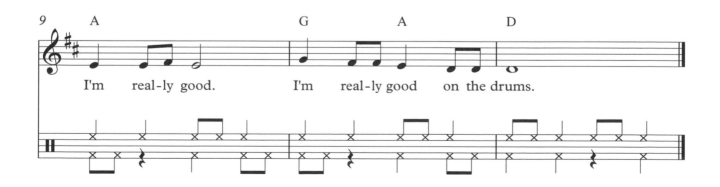

Don't You Brag

Thornton Cline

The Man In The Music Store

Thornton Cline

♩=102 Pensive

(snare drums)

(bass drums)

The man in the mu - sic store says my drums will shrink, if

I keep brag - ging a - bout how good I am. The

man in the mu - sic store says you must be hum - ble.

Sure, you're get-ting bet-ter but don't let it get to your head.

37

Your Drums Will Shrink

Thornton Cline

♩=100 **Cautious**

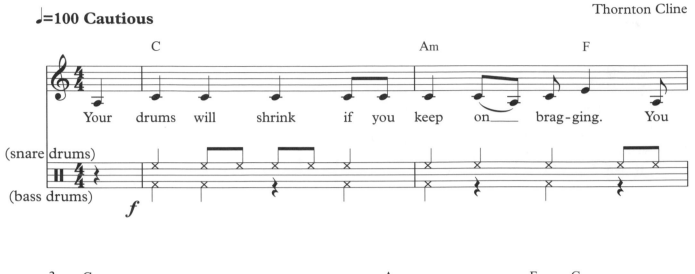

(snare drums)

(bass drums)

f

Your drums will shrink if you keep on___ brag-ging. You

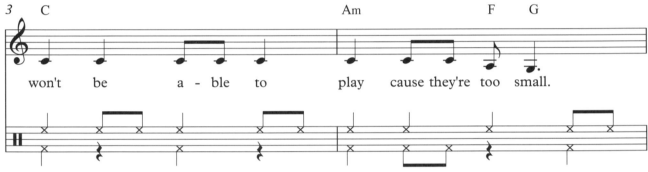

won't be a - ble to play cause they're too small.

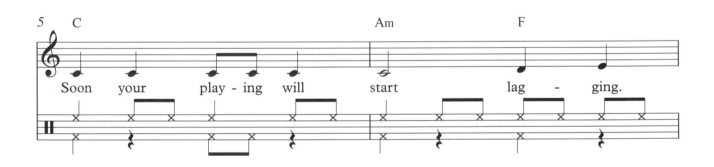

Soon your play - ing will start lag - ging.

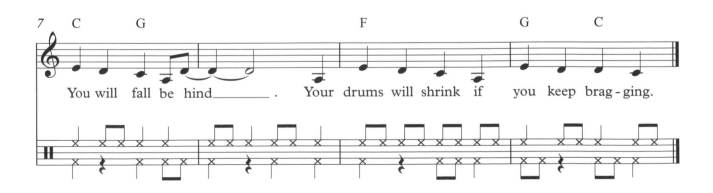

You will fall be hind_____ . Your drums will shrink if you keep brag-ging.

Could The Man Be Right?

Got To Get My Drums Back

Thornton Cline

♩=102 **Yearning**

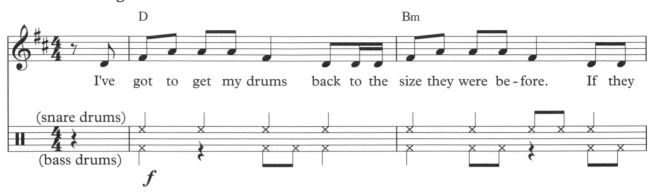

I've got to get my drums back to the size they were be-fore. If they

(snare drums)

(bass drums)

_f_

keep on shrink-ing, I won't be play-ing a-ny more I've

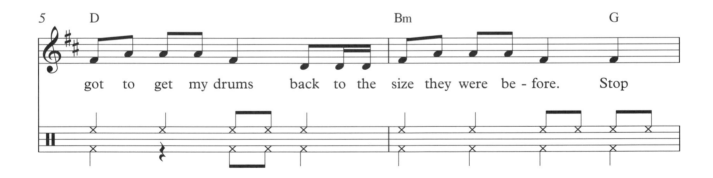

got to get my drums back to the size they were be-fore. Stop

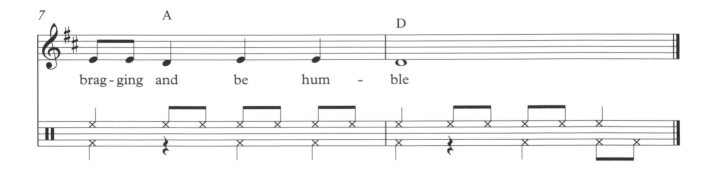

brag-ging and be hum - ble

I Can Play My Drums Again

Thornton Cline

Thank You

Thornton Cline

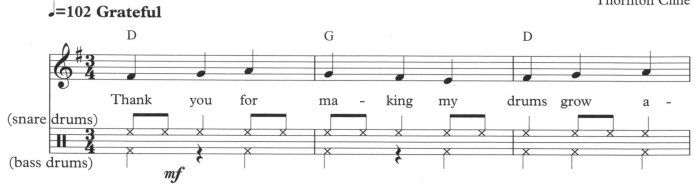

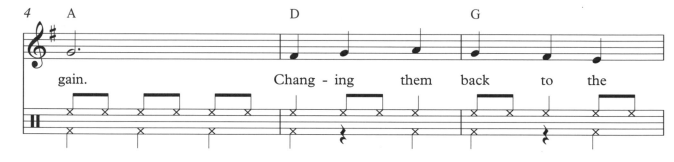

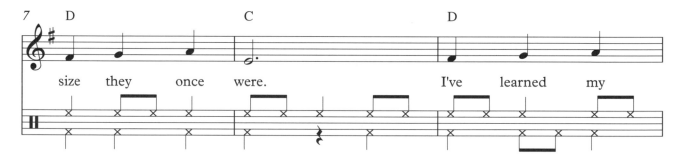

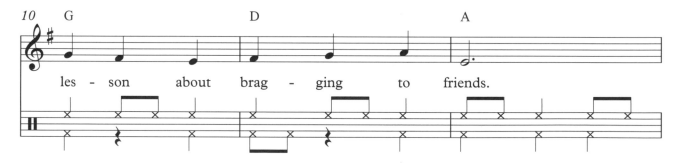

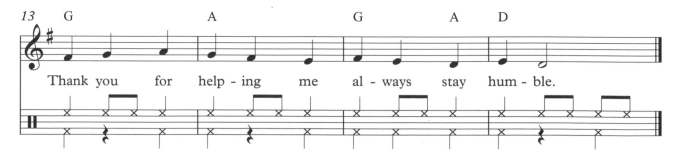

The Way I've Changed

Thornton Cline

43

Biographies

Thornton Cline is author of thirteen books: *Band of Angels, Practice Personalities: What's Your Type? Practice Personalities for Adults, The Contrary, The Amazing Incredible Shrinking Violin, The Amazing Incredible Shrinking Piano, The Amazing Incredible Shrinking Guitar, The Amazing Musical Magical Plants, A Travesty of Justice, Not My Time to Go, The Amazing Incredible Shrinking Ukulele, Perfectly Precious Poolichious,* and Cline's seventh children's book, *The Amazing Incredible Shrinking Drums.* Thornton Cline has been honored with "Songwriter of the Year" twice in a row by the Tennessee Songwriter's Association for his hit song, "Love is the Reason," recorded by Engelbert Humperdinck and Gloria Gaynor. Cline has received Dove and Grammy Award nominations for his songs. Thornton Cline is an in-demand author, teacher, speaker, clinician, performer and songwriter. He lives in Hendersonville, Tennessee with his wife, Audrey.

Susan Oliver is an award-winning songwriter and visual artist as well as illustrator. She is originally from Orono, Maine and attended the University of Maine as well as Portland School of Art. Known for her wide variety of styles, Susan has exhibited her artwork and also worked as a graphic designer. Her painting, "Moonlight Seals" gained national attention in efforts to raise funds for Marine Animal Lifeline, an organization dedicated to seal rescue and rehabilitation. Susan now resides outside of Nashville, Tennessee where she continues to write music and design art work for album covers for various musical artists, as well as illustrates children's books. *The Amazing Incredible Shrinking Drums* is Oliver's sixth children's book published as an illustrator.

Credits

Audrey

Alex Cline

Mollie Cline

God

Ron Middlebrook

Centerstream/Hal Leonard

Susan Oliver

Crystal Bowman

Sumner Academy

Cumberland Arts Academy

Cumberland University

Marcelo Cataldo, transcriber

Hendersonville Christian Academy

Clinetel Music

Gallatin Creative Arts Center

Lawrence Boothby, photographer

Another Amazing Book!

"The rousing climax will delight and entertain all"
– Nancy and Randall Faber

"Sweet story, well written"!
– Marlene Tachoir

THE AMAZING MAGICAL MUSICAL PLANTS

Story by Thornton Cline & Crystal Bowman, Illustrations by Susan Oliver

Mr. Jones is having trouble motivating his fifth grade band students to practice. When he discovers a packet of magical musical plant seeds in an old trombone case, he gets an idea. Mr. Jones plants the seeds in pots of soil and gives one to each of his students to take home. He tells the students how to care for the seeds and to play their instruments every day to make the plants grow. Some of his students laugh at his crazy idea, but some of his students take him seriously. The whimsical illustrations by acclaimed illustrator Susan Oliver add to the charm of this delightful story. The book includes a CD of ten easy original songs with recorded examples of each instrument. (Recommended for ages 4-8)

00155787 Book/CD Pack...$19.99

P.O. Box 17878 - Anaheim Hills, CA 92817

(714) 779-9390   www.centerstream-usa.com

More Amazing Books!

THE AMAZING INCREDIBLE SHRINKING VIOLIN
00142509 Book/CD Pack.................................. $19.99

THE AMAZING INCREDIBLE SHRINKING PIANO
00149098 Book/CD Pack.................................. $19.99

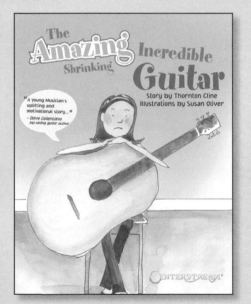

THE AMAZING, INCREDIBLE, SHRINKING GUITAR
00159517 .... $9.99

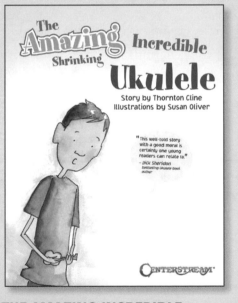

THE AMAZING INCREDIBLE SHRINKING UKULELE
00194560.. $9.99

P.O. Box 17878 - Anaheim Hills, CA 92817

(714) 779-9390   www.centerstream-usa.com

More Great Books from Thornton Cline...

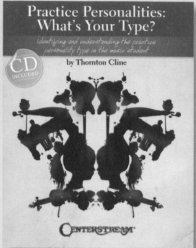